T0146983

LESSONS FROM

Nature

Reflections, Poems and Prayers
Inspired by Creation

KATHY ROY

LESSONS FROM NATURE
REFLECTIONS, POEMS AND PRAYERS
INSPIRED BY CREATION

Copyright © 2019 Kathy Roy.
Photo Imagery: © Kathy Roy
Cover Image: © Tammy Patterson
Editor: Laura Klein

Spirit Garden Books
PO Box 24008 LANCASTER
Saint John NB E2M 5R8
Canada

Scripture quotations marked NRSV are taken from the New Revised Standard Version of the Bible, Copyright © 1989, by the Division of Christian Education of the National Council of the Churches of Christ in the United States of America. Used by permission. All rights reserved. Website

iUniverse books may be ordered through booksellers or by contacting:

iUniverse
1663 Liberty Drive
Bloomington, IN 47403
www.iuniverse.com
1-800-Authors (1-800-288-4677)

ISBN: 978-1-5320-7472-1 (sc)
ISBN: 978-1-5320-7471-4 (e)

Library of Congress Control Number: 2019906512

Print information available on the last page.

iUniverse rev. date: 07/09/2019

Contents

Praise for Lessons from Nature

"The reflections Kathy offers in Lessons from Nature are deeply nourishing and calming and take me back to deep and simple truths - truths that seem to course through my body - realigning me with all that is. There is Divine wisdom and guidance on every page."

Liz Garratt, Founder of Harmony by Design

www.harmonybydesign.ca

"Read this book. These are words that guide the heart. Kathy shares her nature experiences with a gentle honesty and vulnerable spirit. You'll meet playful seals, patient spiders, succulent cactus, yielding snow, strong butterflies and persistent rivers. These are Kathy's friends and teachers. You sense her respect. You see a heart open to wonder, wisdom and change. You'll learn to listen, to deeply notice, and come to your senses. These are wisdom teachings from one steeped in interfaith practice. Read this book. Read this book outdoors if you can. Here is support for everyday mystics."

Janice MacLean, Founder of The Prayer Bench

www.prayerbench.ca

Dedication

In gratitude for the gifts of
earth,
sea,
and
sky.

Introduction

Nature has always been my teacher. In the pages of this book, you will find reflections on the lessons I have learned from spending time in nature. It has been my experience that observing and listening to nature often mirrors back to me some aspect of my inner landscape. Time in nature is a time of revelation, inspiration and, often, consolation.

It is no wonder that in the Celtic tradition, it is said that there are two books of revelation: one is the written word of scriptures and the other is creation. This has been my experience. It is to nature that I turn when my heart is searching and seeking. It is in nature that I feel the closest to my Creator. It is in nature that my heart falls open to with receptivity to the generosity of the Beloved. When immersing myself in nature, every bush becomes a burning bush. Every plant, every stone, every tree, every body of water has secrets to share and reveal.

It has taken me many years to muster the courage to share some of the reflections I have written of my time in nature. Yet, when I have shared what I have written with others, the stories often spark something within the reader. They remember their own experiences, their own lessons, their own insights that nature has shared with them.

My hope is that, as you read these reflections, they might evoke something within you. Perhaps they spark a memory or an insight; or take you deeper into your own experiences of nature's revelations. Perhaps they draw you closer to the heart of creation; and perhaps they inspire you. It is not mine to know how these reflections will affect you.

It is simply my call to share what nature has gifted to me in the hopes that the gifts might grow.

Many of these reflections have been written over a ten-year period of my own inner growth and transformation process. In compiling these reflections, I notice that there are themes among the writing: letting go, being willing to change, practicing stillness, patience, waiting and allowing inner restoration to happen. These writings are ones that have helped me integrate a way of living that flows with the natural rhythms of life unfolding.

In allowing nature to be my teacher, I have come to appreciate the movement of the elements in my day-to-day life. It is no surprise that almost every wisdom tradition speaks of the elements in some manner as a metaphor to describe the Sacred. Earth, air, water and fire all have their own movement and impact upon our living that deepens, transforms and teaches. You will find that the reflections in this book are offered in sections that correspond with the elements.

As you read, you may be inspired to ponder how the Sacred moves through the elements to support and nurture your own life. You may become more aware of how the earth grounds you, how the air creates movement in your life, how water teaches you to flow, and how fire brings passion, light and transformation to your life.

As a spiritual director and interfaith minister, I have spent years holding space for others as they explore their connection to the Divine. Throughout this book, you will notice that some reflections end with a question, a poem, a scripture reading, or a blessing. This is my way of holding space for you to listen to what is arising in your own soul as you read. Occasionally, you will see a picture incorporated into a reflection. Many of us have heard the saying that a picture is worth a thousand words. Images are the language of the soul and their evocative nature can stir our heart and bring forth new awareness. May you use these questions, poems, prayers and images as an invitation to listen to what is stirring within you as you read.

It is my hope that you will pick up *Lessons from Nature* on the days that you just need a little something to speak to your heart. May you crack the book open to a page that is exactly what you need to read on that day.

From the lessons, teachings and wisdom nature has gifted to me, I now pass the gifts along to you.

Blessings,
Kathy Roy

Earth

A desert stretching,
A beach inviting,
A prairie field, grasses waving,
A mountain rising,
A cave sheltering,
A meadow of green,
A garden of abundance.

Restoration

I am staying with a friend in Castlemartyr, Ireland and I went this morning to visit the garden behind the house. Carrying a stool and a shawl, I walked across the grass to sit near the trees. It is a wonderful thing to have such privacy in the garden and I am grateful for the stone walls that make me feel safe. I am grateful for the empty green pasture that lies straight in front of me, and I am grateful for the line of trees that grow tall and thick between me and the neighbour. This garden is an oasis of privacy that allows me to connect deeply with nature.

I sit on my stool and listen to the sounds of the birds flying overhead, the birdsongs coming from hidden places in the trees, and the whisper of the wind as it rustles the leaves of the trees. Soon, sitting in nature is not enough. My whole being longs to stretch out upon the surface of the earth and lie down with my face turned up toward the sun. My body feels almost boneless as it melts off the stool and slides into the cool blanket of grass. It has been too long since I have lain like this upon the earth. To do so now feels like a reunion of a kind I cannot quite put my finger on. It is as though something that was missing has now been found. I am laying in a green pasture and I am finding a restoration that fills the depths of me.

In these days of rapid movement, agendas and deadlines, it is a rare thing to find time to simply lie down in a field and listen. I find my ears adjusting to the slower rhythm of listening to nature. The penetrating warmth of the sun helps me discover the many places in my face, neck and shoulders that hold stress and strain. Slowly, the sun lifts these burdens and restores my muscles to liquid, sensuous softness.

I continue to sink deeper into the embrace of the grass and I feel the solid earth beneath me. The contrasting sensations of the cool dampness of the earth along my back and the warmth of the sun on the front of my body help my whole being relax even further. I don't want to move. I feel the weight of my own presence in every limb and am aware of being very much alive. I am alive with *being* - not with doing. I wonder, sometimes, if my need to accomplish and achieve is simply a means of proving to myself that I exist. Yet, in this moment of surrendering fully to presence, I recognize life in a more satisfying way. The ancient depths of my soul know I am more alive in this moment than I am when I am busy accomplishing the tasks of the day. In this moment, I am in harmony with the natural world. I remember that I am a part of nature.

I hear a bumble bee flying around me, drinking from the wildflowers hidden in the grass. The sound of its humming is comforting. As the bee flies away, I sink back into a moment of silence before the next sound calls my attention. Even with my eyes closed, I make out the distinctive sound of a pigeon flapping its wings overhead. I relax even further as I begin to realize that I instinctively recognize these sounds, even with my eyes closed. I am more in tune with nature than I thought. It is a relief to recognize this. I can breathe deeper. I am coming home to myself and my place in the unfolding story of creation.

There is a deep restoration of my soul as I lie in this green pasture. There is a remembering of who I am and a recognition of my kinship with the natural world. The butterflies, bees, flowers and birds seem to make space for me to join them. They do not look at me and think I am separate from nature. Only I forget that nature and I are one. Their wisdom is deeper than my own. Lying in green pastures is about returning to my place as a child of the earth.

As I lie in this field, I feel my heart begin to expand. It becomes easier to breathe. I hope I can remember this moment in the days and months to follow. I hope I allow myself to be called back to lay upon the earth and receive this kind of deep restoration. I am not meant to stand two-footed and scurry around all the time.

I have read the 23rd Psalm many times in my life. It is unfortunate that I have associated it so deeply with funerals, for in this moment, I realize the psalm is more about life than death. It is about restoration of the soul. My prayer is to live it more consistently, less sporadically, so that my flesh and bones, as well as my spirit, know the gift of restoration.

I laid upon the earth for more than two hours but the time seemed to float by in my awareness. I believe I learned something new about rest: I do not have to slumber to be restored. I must surrender and open myself to the blessing of restoration. In lying with my face to the sun, I let go of resistance, tension and stress. This is restoration.

"The Lord is my shepherd, I shall not want.
He makes me lie down in green pastures;
He leads me beside still waters;
He restores my soul.
He leads me in right paths
For his name's sake."
Psalm 23:1–3

What brings you a sense of restoration?

Daughter of the Earth

I am on retreat and we have just finished a ceremony to enter into a time of Sabbath. As a community, we will be holding 24 hours of silence together. I am so grateful for the shared silence, for the opportunity to turn inward and to listen for the voice of the Sacred.

For the last few days, I have been holding the question, "What does it mean to be made in the image of God?" In this time of silence, I am opening myself to discover what this truly means in my own life. I need something I can relate to, something that speaks to my heart, opens my eyes and helps me live in accordance with this longing I feel to allow the Sacred into my life more fully. It is a longing to know, a longing to surrender, a longing for union.

I am so grateful for this circle of silence that provides me with heightened awareness and an openness to being touched by the Mystery we live in. The silence brings relief, comfort and an awareness that I am prepared to listen; I am prepared to receive.

As I enter my room and reach for my journal, words are ready to come forth in response to the question living in my heart. These words pour onto the page as if they have simply been waiting for an invitation:

Daughter of the Earth,
Can you hear me calling?
I am the quickening in your spirit
Beckoning for your company.

Daughter of the Earth,
Come greet me with your presence.
I long to spend time with you.
Come sit with me and delight in my greenness.

Daughter of the Earth,
Do you feel me calling?
You know who I am.
I have been waiting for you.

Daughter of the Earth,
You are created in my image.
The deep colour of your hair,
The pinkness of your skin,
The green shimmer of your eyes are echoes of me.
You are my daughter and I am calling you to life.

Daughter of the Earth,
Can you feel it?
The core of molten power churning with
Life deep within you?

Daughter of the Earth,
Can you feel the wildness within you?
To live wild is to be free to roam, explore,
play, work, and live with abandon and freedom.

Daughter of the Earth,
Can you feel my rivers coursing through your veins?
My rivers bring refreshment, life, and movement.

Daughter of the Earth,
I beckon you to greet me with your embrace.
My trees sway with encouragement.

My grasses whisper in invitation.
My birds sing with sweet welcome.

Daughter of the Earth,
I am your Mother.
Over the years I have watched you grow.
I have kissed your cheeks with the sun.
I have stroked your hair with the wind.
I have cleansed you with my rain.
I have supported your feet as you dance.
I have soaked up your tears when you cry.

Daughter of the Earth,
I have marked you as mine.
I have claimed you.

Daughter of the Earth,
I have called you because you are ready.
Your rite of passage has ended.

Daughter of the Earth,
We now walk as one.
Vibrant, colourful, glorious.
Each step you place upon my surface is a step we make together.

Daughter of the Earth,
We stand united in strength,
Softness,
Firmness.

Daughter of the Earth,
Recognize through my image
That many faces are called for in nurturing life.
Crustiness.

Hardness.
Softness.
Moistness.
Dryness.
Deepness.
Rockiness.
Flatness.
Richness.

Daughter of the Earth.
Let's begin.

These words come fast and swift, as though they had been waiting a long time for me to welcome them. Tears well in my eyes. Something echoes in my soul as a recognition of the life that I am part of. I am not separate from anything. I am not alone. I am part of an interconnected whole with the natural world around me. The Mystery that made me is living in me, pulsing in me, flowing in me. This recognition and quickening in my spirit flows out on the page in response:

I am daughter of the Earth, and your call resounds within me.
My whole being recognizes it's origin in you.

You have filled my heart with your molten lava of Life.
Like you, this liquid passion is buried deep within my centre,
supporting the life of my ever-increasing layers.

I recognize you in the green reflection of my eyes,
which resemble the depths of the sea.
In my eyes, you have placed the shimmer of wet leaves
and the moistness of moss.

I see you in the dye which you have cast upon my hair.
Deep hues of brown that refract the colours of your surface.

I AM daughter of the Earth.
I have sought comfort in your soft blanket of grasses.
I have found delight in your vibrant array of flowers.
I have learned from your creatures.
I have been refreshed by your breeze
And have felt you quake beneath my feet.

I am daughter of the Earth.
Your strength surges through me.
I claim the right to:
Wildness
Firmness
Strength
Softness
Greenness
Gentleness

I am daughter of the Earth.
Dappled with Rain.
Kissed by the Sun.
Moved by the Wind.
Ready to Begin.

As the flow of words ebbs, I am left with a feeling of relief. It is a feeling that at last I know who I am. I walk outside to sit on the grass overlooking the river and everything seems brighter, greener and more alive than I have ever seen it before.

The earth is full of nurturing, giving, love, abundance, potential, regeneration, tenacity and miracles of forgiveness. I am made in the image of this bounty. For many years, I have grappled on and off with the question of what it means to be made in the image of God. With the outpouring of this poem, a new image has been revealed to me. It is vibrantly alive and loving, and it grounds me instantly when I think of it. The molten core of the earth is the same as the molten core of my heart. Within these twin cores lies the desire to continue bringing forth creation out of a need to express love. The essence within me mirrors the essence in God and all creation: generosity and love.

What does it mean to you to be made in the image of God?

Watchful Waiting

While sitting outside on my deck, I look up and I notice that a spider has built a web between two spindles in the deck railing. The intricacy and beauty of the web has caught my attention. I always marvel that spiders can weave webs that are so strong, yet look so delicate.

As I gaze at the web, it takes a moment before my eyes can locate the spider. Then I see it tucked up in the right-hand corner of the web, half hidden by a branch on the cedar tree. It is sitting upside down and very still. It makes me think, "This is what relaxing and waiting looks like." The spider is just hanging out in its web. Watching it makes me settle down and feel more stillness within myself.

Suddenly, a fly lands on the web and the whole thing begins to quake and shiver. In a flash, the spider has gone from stillness to motion. Within seconds, almost as fast as I can blink, the spider has immobilized the fly by wrapping webbing around it. As soon as the fly is subdued, the spider goes back up to its corner and sits in stillness.

I am amazed at the quickness and deftness of the spider, its state of watchful waiting. It was at rest, yet it was also ready to move when life brought it a fly.

As I am pondering this spider and its web, I catch a flash of something moving in the field across the road. The neighbour's cat has found a mouse to hunt in the grass. The cat is stalking the mouse and then racing all over the field giving chase to it. Then it stops, hunkers down low to the ground, watching and wiggling its back end in anticipation of the next chase. Moments later, it is off again, racing around the field.

I am struck by the difference between the spider and the cat. Each is hunting prey, they just go about it very differently. The spider spins a web to catch its prey. It sits in a very restful state and waits, trusting that, eventually, a bug will land in the web.

The cat, on the other hand, is still racing around the field, chasing after its prey. It is enjoying stalking the mouse. I don't know if it will ever catch it, but it is certainly preoccupied with the chase.

The spider and the cat are my teachers at this moment. As I watch how each one behaves, I feel like life wants me to learn something from them. As I sit in the sun, pondering what I am witnessing, I realize the lesson is this: *"Life will come to you, you don't always have to chase after it."*

These words bring me a sense of peace. I am being invited to be more like the spider and to practice watchful waiting, trusting that life will bring me what I need. Watching the spider and the cat, I am reminded of this traditional tale:

> *Rabbi Levi saw a man running in the street, and asked him, "Why do you run?" He replied, "I am running after my good fortune!" Rabbi Levi tells him, "Silly man, your good fortune has been trying to chase you, but you are running too fast."*[1]

We don't have to chase after life, it knows where to find us. Our job is to open to it with receptivity.

While writing this reflection, I had a phone conversation with a friend that exemplified watchful waiting. She shared with me that she has held a yearning in her heart to minister in some way to women who have lost a child due to premature birth or miscarriages. She has held

---

[1] Muller, Wayne. *Sabbath: Finding Rest, Renewal, and Delight in Our Busy Lives.* New York, New York: Bantam Books, 2000.

this yearning for over twenty-five years. Then, out of the blue, she is reading a story in the local newspaper about a new venture starting up that offers grief support to women who have lost a child in this way. My friend realizes - this is it. This is the opportunity she has been looking for and she moved into action and got in touch with the organization.

This is watchful waiting.

We have a yearning and we don't know how it will be met or when, but the yearning helps us be ready and prepared to act when life presents an opportunity to us. We don't chase the opportunity, we practice watchful waiting.

Stop Playing with the Boulder

The words, "Stop playing with the boulder," keep coming to me. These words help me recognize how often I become preoccupied with the boulder that seems to be blocking my path. In my preoccupation, I don't see all the wide open spaces around me into which I could move. Instead, I see only the boulder, I push at the boulder; I try to pick it up; I try to move it. I give all of my strength to trying to budge the boulder.

My guidance is clear: leave the boulder alone and move to where life is flowing freely. Living near the ocean, I know that boulders don't stop the tide from coming in. The ocean flows around the boulders. This is what my guidance is saying. Become more like water and flow around the boulders. There are other ways to move forward. I do not have to be preoccupied with the boulder that seems to be in the way.

It makes me laugh every time I think of the words, "Stop playing with the boulder." We can leave the boulders in our lives alone sometimes; we do not have to push and strain so hard. If we were to take our eyes off the boulder, we may find other avenues to explore.

I am known in my family for being stubborn. I tend to get focused on a goal and not give up until I make it. I can tell that it is my ego that gets so stuck on playing with the boulders along my path. My ego seems to be finely tuned to focusing on where I *can't* go as opposed to looking up and seeing all the places that I can move freely.

It is okay to walk away from the boulder sometimes. The big things in our lives will move and shift when they are ready to. For now, I am listening to my inner wisdom, walking away from the boulder, and finding something more life-giving to play with.

By no means am I saying that we should walk away from doing our inner work. I am just recognizing that sometimes I get mired down in the weight of the boulders when, perhaps, I don't have to. I can trust that if the way isn't opening and it is blocked with boulders right now, then it is not the time or the place for me to be walking. If the boulder won't roll away when I try to push it, then I can try going a different way, or wait for a different time.

In the Quaker tradition, they speak of Way opening and Way closing. This concept of our path draws us into a place of deep acceptance. It helps us listen and watch for where Way is opening and to trust when Way is closing. This wisdom calls us to live in the natural ebb and flow of life.

I think that many of us tire ourselves out by playing with our boulders, trying to push what we perceive as blocks out of our way and trying to force Way to open. For today, I am going to leave my boulders alone and stop pushing. I know what they are, I know they are there, and I am choosing to go play in areas of my life that naturally flow and allow life to move forward. I am choosing to place myself where Way is opening. I choose to trust that the boulder will let me know when, and if, it is ready to roll away.

What are the boulders that you are trying to
push out of the way right now?
What would happen if you left the boulder alone for a while and
turned your focus to where flow is happening in your life?
Take your life energy and play there today.

An Invitation to Change

Standing under the branches of a large oak tree I feel sheltered and embraced. The warmth of the sun filters through the branches and the leaves. I have come outside to enjoy some time with this beautiful tree while facilitating a retreat.

I have given the participants the invitation to "come to their senses" and spend some time outdoors, listening to nature. I felt called to take a few moments for myself and have stepped outside to be with this tree. I want to feel the roots of the tree connecting me to the earth, so I ask her permission to step in a little closer and I begin to feel her energy and her embrace.

I have taken my shoes off and stand here with bare feet sunk in the grass. Mosquitoes are biting my ankles, but it feels so good to stand near this tree that I don't mind.

Looking out over the grassy hill, I take in the view of the river flowing below. As I watch the river, the desire to unfold and flow like this ribbon of water is felt deep in my gut. I have a feeling of being ready to blossom. I am ready to unfurl, to expand and be more than I have been before.

After a moment, I lift my gaze from the river and peer up through the branches of my tree companion. Her leaves have begun to change as summer gives itself over to fall. One leaf catches my attention. It is perforated with little holes. I stare at it and feel these words dance through my awareness: *"Be willing to change."*

This leaf still has its outer shape and is vibrantly green, yet it has been eaten by a bug of some sort, making it permeable. It is beautiful in this changed shape. As I look at it, the sun is shining through each little hole on its surface, making the leaf look like lace.

When it is time to go back into the retreat centre, I carry the image of this leaf with me. The invitation to be willing to change stays with me, it stings my eyes and touches my heart. The leaf evoked an ache in me that I didn't even know was there. I have a longing for something in my life to change. I have a longing to be less and more at the same time, like this leaf that has had some parts removed in order to let the sun shine through and reveal its delicate lace-like nature. I am ready to let go of something so that I can become more of myself, so that I can let the light shine through me.

A few days later, the image of that leaf is very much with me. I can close my eyes and see it clearly. I recall how the mystic Hildegard de Bingen said that we are bearers of light. I sense that my soul knows this and it wants to create more and more space within me so that the light can shine. I want to be porous, like that leaf. I want to retain my shape, but to change enough that the light can shine through me and radiate beauty.

I am willing to change. I am willing to be like the trees and their leaves, I am willing to blossom, to stop holding on so tightly. I am willing to open and be more generous with myself. I am willing to be radiant.

Be willing to change.
Be willing to let go of what is not needed.
Be willing to transform.
Be willing.

The leaf has taught me that to be more, I can also be less. I can live into this paradox of being less dense, less fearful, less full of myself, so that I can be lighter, freer, more spacious. I can be more whole by being less. This is my invitation to change.

Be the Vessel

As I sat down to do my morning practice of gratitude and meditation, I was reflecting on how grateful I am for choosing to live simply. I was feeling my heart well up with gratitude for the gifts that aligning myself with simplicity have offered me, and I felt tears fill my eyes. Tears are the way that I know I have touched on something important to my soul.

I sat with the feeling for a few moments and my gaze fell upon a vase on my bookshelf. The vase was a gift from my wedding, but I have never found anything to put in it. It is a simple pottery vase and I had always felt it was a shame that I didn't use it or have an arrangement in it.

Today, as my meditative gaze took in the vase, the words "empty spaces are prepared and ready to receive" came to me. A warm flush moved its way through my heart. I knew this was an important message about simplicity. I also knew that the vase was a reflection of myself. When I empty myself of the thoughts that clutter up my mind, I become a clear vessel that is ready to receive new insights and inspirations. When I can hold this space, even for a few seconds, an insight that feeds my soul can come to me. That is what happened this morning. The message that empty spaces are prepared and ready to receive is like a balm to my soul that has nourished the life within me. These words are an affirmation that my desire to live a life of simple abundance is the exact right choice for me.

In the few seconds in which all of this took place, I came to a much deeper understanding that I do not have to fill each moment of my day. I need empty spaces, because it is in these empty spaces that my soul becomes fertile and prepared to receive inspiration, insight and sustenance from the Sacred.

So, I returned my gaze to the empty vase on my bookshelf, giving thanks for its emptiness and the symbol that it has now become of being the empty container that is prepared, ready and waiting to receive.

Empty spaces are prepared and ready to receive.

Erosion

While walking on the beach, I hear the waves crashing to the right of me. It is a sound that is calming and reassuring for me. There is a consistency to the sound of the waves breaking on the shore that helps my breathing settle and deepen.

Opposite the waves is a high cliff face of rich brown earth, stones and tree roots, with grass, bushes and trees growing along the top of the ridge. I stand for a moment, in awe of the colour and contrast the cliff gives to the sand on the beach.

It is when I stop to look at the cliff that I hear it, the sound of rocks giving way and tumbling down the side of the cliff's face. Something in my stomach shifts with recognition at this sound. It echoes with a sensation I have been feeling lately, a sensation of something sliding away from me.

As I listen to the cliff, I have a sense of how easy it is to let go. The cliff seems to simply release pieces of itself and send earth, rock and pebbles tumbling down to the beach below.

I know I am witnessing erosion, but I am not feeling sad about the cliff giving way to the influence the crashing waves have had on it. Instead, I feel a sense of hope. I am watching and witnessing transformation taking place. The shape and structure of this cliff is changing because of the air, the water, and the influence of the environment around it. Who am I to say that the change is good or bad?

I realize that I have been resisting change. I feel something eroding within me and I want to cling rather than release. Something is beginning to fall away and I am not sure I want it to. Listening to the cliff I begin to wonder, "What if I surrendered to change, the way the cliff does? What if I allowed the shape of my inner life to be transformed? What if I willingly let go?"

I am aware that there is a yearning in my soul for this kind of letting go. Perhaps there is an inner facade that is ready to crumble and reveal more of my true nature. What if, in letting go, nothing is being lost but rather transformed and sculpted into its true beauty?

I look at the cliff in a whole new way now. I am grateful for this lesson it has given me. It has been my teacher, showing me that I can choose to let go. Erosion is an on-going process that changes the face of the earth. It is an on-going process that changes my inner landscape as well.

> *Release.*
> *Let Go.*
> *Stones bounce and tumble*
> *landing on the beach below.*
> *Transformation.*
> *It is on-going work*
> *that leads to*
> *revelation.*

When being sculpted by the Sculptor, be gentle. The cliff is not being transformed in one day. It is a slow process. The earth is shifting, changing, letting go, releasing. Change is inevitable. It is on-going. Sometimes it happens so slowly you cannot detect it. Then, one day, you open your eyes and the landscape has shifted. You are standing in a new place. This kind of transformation is happening within each of us. You can't rush it, but you can cooperate with it.

I left the beach feeling oddly hopeful after listening to the cliff. My sense of erosion is no longer about damage but, instead, a shifting of the landscape, a sculpting and shaping that is an inevitable part of life. I can live with it more easily now as I sense it happening within me. It is a letting go of what is not needed.

Nothing in creation is exempt from the effects of change and transformation; we can resist, but we cannot stop it. Like the Grand Canyon, we can be transformed from one form of beauty into another.

What are you being invited to release? In what ways might you cooperate with the energy of transformation?

Planting Seeds

Spring is a season that teaches me about patience and waiting. I have an inner sense of anticipation and a readiness to see the snow melt and flowers begin to blossom, yet I am called to pause and wait when the warming weather suddenly turns back into grey clouds and falling snow. Spring is a season that I have come to name as the time of "not yet". Like many others, I can feel spring long before I have evidence that it is actually here. The spring calls me to mindfully practice patience while nurturing my desire to be outdoors digging in the earth and planting seeds.

The call I feel to be planting seeds is both metaphorical and a real desire to garden and grow food in my backyard. There is something about sowing seeds and then watching the plants grow that teaches us about waiting and having patience until the seedlings grow and produce blossoms that turn into fruit. Planting seeds reminds me that any growth, any change, any transition takes time to root itself and become established before the blossoms can be revealed.

One morning, I awakened before the first light of dawn with the word *bamboo* echoing in my mind. I had fallen asleep the night before wondering about when I would ever see some of my dreams and goals become reality. I knew that the word *bamboo* was an answer to my question.

The legend of Chinese bamboo says that it takes five years after planting the seed before any sign of life emerges above the ground. During those five years, the seed is working underground to establish a strong and solid root system that will support the plant. Once the shoot breaks through the ground, the stock can grow up to 80 feet high in a very short amount of time. The plant must have a solid root system to support this kind of growth.

The word *bamboo* has become a mantra for me this month. It is a reminder that the seeds of my dreams take time to establish themselves - they do not blossom immediately. There are "dream seeds" I planted ten years ago that are just beginning to show signs of growth. Yet, in those ten years, the soil of my heart, mind and spirit have been nurtured, watered and tended to through prayer, meditation, and a willingness to pull the weeds of some old belief systems that would severely hamper the ability of my dreams to flourish.

For many of us, our biggest dreams require patience, faith and perseverance in order for them to grow. Our goals may also entail struggle and growth in order for our inner landscape to support the root system of the dream we are building.

Spring always comes as a reminder not to give up on my dreams. Where I live, this season starts off dirty and barren looking, but it always ends with tulips growing in my front garden and blossoms appearing on the trees. Somewhere in the middle, the songbirds return and brighten the day with their singing. A season that begins by looking drab and lifeless always ends in a riot of spectacular colour and beauty. Blossoming is the hope of spring.

May you trust that your own dreams will blossom in their right
time, just like spring brings forth her beauty in her own time.
May you be fortified with strength and perseverance, patience
and faith as you watch over your own field of dreams.
May you trust that every struggle and every lesson you
experience is helping to establish a root system strong
enough to support the dreams you have planted.

I Want to Care for This

Every year, I go on a silent retreat as part of my commitment to living the contemplative path. I always choose a place that is secluded and nestled into nature. This time, I rented a home near Peggy's Cove, Nova Scotia with beautiful walking trails and views of the Atlantic Ocean.

I was entering the silence to prepare myself for crossing the threshold into ministry. I had been studying the mystical heart of the world's wisdom traditions for the past two years and was about to be ordained as an interfaith/interspiritual minister.

There was a question that I carried with me into the silence: How then shall I live? This question had been echoing in my heart as ordination approached and I looked forward to this time of silence and reflection to hold it prayerfully.

When I arrived at the house, I parked in the driveway and was about to get out of my car when I saw a rustling in the trees in front of me. The face of a deer emerged from behind the branches. This beautiful animal was having its dinner and, when it saw me, it stopped and stared. It must have determined that I wasn't much of a threat because it soon went back to munching leaves while I watched. I have always had an affinity for deer and being so close to this one was a gift. I felt awed into silence, thus beginning my retreat.

It didn't take me long to discover that this house I was settling into was, first and foremost, home to a number of deer. The house was surrounded by windows and I could watch the deer, five in all, come wandering out of the woods at the back of the house, munching on leaves as they meandered to the front where there were tender bushes to dine on. The deer brought with them a reminder of gentleness and compassion. When they drew close enough, I was able to see their eyes and could feel the gentleness of their spirit. Yet these deer were not skittish. When I went out on the deck to watch them, the youngest one turned to me and stamped its front hoof firmly on the ground as if to say, "This is mine." It was easy to agree. This was the deer's land. They knew it inside and out and I was but a guest.

This feeling of being the guest of nature stayed with me throughout my retreat. One morning, I woke very early and watched the sun rise over the water. I went out for a walk and sat on the rocks by the sea. A duck was also awake to greet the day and swam a few feet from me, periodically diving under the water to feed. To my right, a heron stood perfectly still. He, too, was watching for his morning meal. Ripples formed around the duck as it slowly paddled away from me, small circles expanding ever outward. My heart seemed to echo the movement and to grow inside my chest. The communion I felt in this place was softening me, helping me breathe easier and feel more peace.

My final morning, I made myself a cup of coffee and stood at the window looking out over the beauty of the land and ocean. I had enjoyed my time here. I felt fed and nourished by nature, by my meditation and by rest.

The words, "You know what to do," were the only response I had received to my quest to know how I should live. I was a little perplexed by this, because my intellect wanted more direct instructions. Suddenly, as I stood in front of the window gazing outward, I felt a deep outpouring from my heart. It was like my heart poured out over the land, the water, the animals and the people to hold it all in an embrace. This deep welling up and pouring forth was accompanied by more words from deep within: "I want to care for this."

Months later, I am still affected by those words. This is how I am to live - with deep and abiding care for all of creation. I have always loved nature, but something shifted during that retreat. My love for this earth expanded, deepened and transformed. I don't have the exact words to describe it. The moment was a humble outpouring while at the same time a deep filling up took place. I felt awash with love for it all.

The gifts that arise out of these times of silent retreat are always deeply soul nourishing. Entering the silence is an invitation to dance with God. I find this dedicated time of silence is my willingness and consent to be "done unto" and surrender my role of being the doer. I like this place of sweet surrender. My soul yearns for it.

I returned home from my retreat to write my vow for ordination. The words formed themselves: "I vow to show up with my heart and to live in service to Love." This is how I shall live.

Heron

Love on the Side of the Road

I saw love on the side of the highway today and it pierced my heart. As I was cruising down the highway, I could see an animal perched on the side of the road. I slowed down as I drew closer and saw that it was a duck. I found this unusual until I noticed that it was perched upon the body of another duck that had been killed by a passing vehicle.

My heart broke open in that moment. This duck had lost its partner and would not leave its side. It covered its companion with its own body, seeking to offer it protection from the oncoming traffic.

My heart instantly recognized the actions of compassion, love and grief I was witnessing on the side of the road.

It made me think of my father-in-law who has been so lovingly tending to my mother-in-law as she succumbs to dementia. There is a loving attentiveness, as well as grief, in his dedication to her.

This is love in action. Standing close to those we love when they need us. Unwilling to part with them when loving gives way to heartache.

This is the side of love that we don't always see. This is the love that hurts, but that the world so desperately needs.

These ducks are my teachers today. They reveal a depth of love and care that touches me deeply. It is hard to witness the destruction our modern lifestyles wreak on nature. I wish I had the powers to restore life to this duck's mate.

I continue to drive with a face wet with tears and my heart aching from witnessing love on the side of the road.

Water

A brook,
A creek,
A river,
An ocean.

A drop,
A mist,
A ripple,
A wave.

Ever changing,
Ever renewing,
Ever creating.

Beach Canvas

I have been walking the beach looking at the captivating mosaic of broken shells and beach stones. There is a random beauty about the way the rocks and shells are dropped in the sand by the receding tide of the ocean. The beach is the ocean's canvas, upon which she leaves artful arrangements of her treasures. Clumps of seaweed create lines that remember the path of the tide. Bits of driftwood have been smoothed and reshaped by the water over time. Jagged rocks have been worn and softened into smooth orbs. Driftwood becomes weathered and more beautiful than any artful design. The ocean delivers these gifts from her body, showing me how rough spots and protective coverings get smoothed away by the waves of time.

The lesson the ocean is showing me is that creativity is a natural emergence that comes from the inner self. I must allow creativity to flow out of me in the random form it wishes and trust that the result will be a beautiful, chaotic and raw expression of my appreciation for life. The process of creation smooths and softens my rough edges.

All too often, before I venture into an act of creativity, I want to be assured that the outcome will be worth the effort. By this, I mean that I want the outcome to be gorgeous, perfect and amazing. This often puts unwarranted pressure on my ability to create and stifles the urge. I then succumb to the fear that my creative efforts will not be perfect and hold myself back from being creative.

The ocean reminds me that creativity calls for abandon. It calls for abandoning judgment and criticism. Stifling creativity is like trying to hold back the tide. Creativity is a natural process that needs to occur for my well-being. The ocean does not judge how it brings in the tide, and I should not judge how my creativity expresses itself. Creativity is a chaotic and explosive process in which ideas bubble to the surface to be carried in on the tide of my thoughts. Allowing the space and freedom for creative ideas and expression to land safely ashore is rewarding and healing.

What is the canvas that catches the gifts of your creative expressions?

Driftwood

Gentle Movements

I have not been at peace today. I have had a sense of inner unrest and disquiet since I woke. My mind is wandering and nagging me with thoughts that are anything but uplifting. My Dad calls this stinky thinking. I had planned to write today, but could not settle enough for words to flow coherently, so I drove to the Nature Park to sit on my favourite rock and let the ocean talk to me.

When I arrived at the parking lot, there was no one else around. The park felt deserted and this made me happy. I wanted to be alone. However, I got no farther than halfway to my favourite rock when another vehicle pulled up and two men got out, an elderly gentleman and his son. In my crankiness, I wished they would turn around and leave. I had come to be alone and to find solace, comfort and softness in nature.

I had some not-very-nice thoughts flowing through my mind as the two men scrambled over rocks and then came to stand directly behind where I had sat down. I could even feel myself mumbling under my breath, "Oh, this is just great." The energy I was giving off was nothing less than rude, but I couldn't even help myself. This is what feeling tired and out of sorts does to me. I had come here seeking solitude because my soul needed quiet and time alone with the rocks and sea. There was a whole beach for these two to wander and it made me cringe that they chose to stand right behind me.

So it surprised me when, upon leaving, the younger man said to me, "Sorry for disturbing your peace." I found myself moved to tears and was grateful for my sunglasses as I smiled at him and said, "It's a beautiful day to be here isn't it?" He agreed and then they left, and I was alone with his words. They hadn't disturbed my peace. I had arrived with my inner peace disturbed. My peace was disturbed by my own mind and thoughts that were rampaging around, creating havoc with my emotions and tilting me off centre. I couldn't see through the cloud my thoughts were creating and had come to this place to seek clarity and peace. This gentleman's words did more to settle my thoughts and help me find my heart again than he will ever know. I am grateful for his kindness and that he was thoughtful enough to say those words when I was most certainly giving off very strong "go away" vibes.

You see, more than just peace began to settle within me with his words. He brought a balm for my soul with his kindness. After they left, I sat for a moment and let the tears flow. His words broke something open inside and now my healing could begin. My mind calmed down and I was able to notice the water. It had been a very windy day up until then, but the wind died down and the tide was flowing out in very slow, calm ripples that seemed to mirror the slow ebbing away of the irritation inside of me. Watching the calm water, I became aware of the need for gentle movements. The ocean was showing me that the tide does not gush out all at once in a forceful way. The tide was moving out in soft little ripples that were barely noticeable. The tide was showing me that it is possible to move great distances with gentle movements. The tide was not trying to go faster than its natural rhythm. It was moving at its own pace, calmly and gently. It was showing me that I do not have to write a book in one fell swoop. I do not have to create with speed. I can move gently, with a rocking rhythm that is soothing, calming and peaceful.

I gave thanks for my lessons and walked back to my car, driving slowly home, carrying peace inside of me, prepared to spend an hour writing from the place of inner calm and connectedness. Once again, Mother Earth had brought me exactly what I needed.

What disrupts your sense of inner peace and throws you
off centre? What gentle movements could you make that
would take you forward in a more natural way?

You Can Relax

I am sitting in church waiting for the service to start, and the words, "You can relax now," rise up within me. These words feel like an invitation to let go and relax into life and to trust that God is with me, helping me and guiding me. I am aware that I hold myself so tensely most of the time, as though I am bracing against life and waiting for the next shoe to drop.

The message, "You can relax now," invites me to let go of thinking I am all alone and to trust that life is unfolding as it should be. I sense deep love and tenderness behind the words and they leave me with a sense that I don't have to work so hard. I am being invited to learn what it means to relax, to nurture myself and to be a good caregiver to my own soul.

As I breathe in the words, "You can relax now," I realize that relaxation is a state of being. It is a state that allows life to flow through you and in you. Relaxation is a state of receptivity. When you relax, you heal yourself. When you relax, you feel a sense of inner contentment and ease. You let go of worry. Relaxation allows the spirit to rest more fully in the body.

To be relaxed is almost to be in a liquid state. It is a way of being fluid from the inside, the opposite of being stiff and solid. Tension and fear create this kind of rigidity in the body and there is a certain mental alertness that lies behind tension. When you relax, you are trusting life, which opens you to a greater sense of receptivity. You recognize the support that is here for you and that you do not hold everything all on your own. When you relax, your focus broadens and you begin to see the larger picture and that there is something greater than you that is helping to shape your life.

Relax and let life flow through you.

Gateway

A friend and I are staying in a house that overlooks the Atlantic Ocean. I cannot believe our good fortune in booking this place. It is a perfect place for retreat. Looking through the living room window, I can see that the tide is going out. I have about an hour before the water recedes enough that I can go for a walk on the beach. Our host has told us that when the tide goes out, a sand bar opens up that will allow us to walk across to a small island. This delights me. It feels like a secret passage and reminds me of the stories I loved as a young girl. We went across to the island yesterday and this morning, I am anxious to walk over again.

Waiting for the tide to go out so I can cross over to the island makes me feel as though I am standing at the threshold of a new adventure. If I have patience and wait, the way will open up for me to move forward.

I realize that when I push forward with my own agenda and neglect to move with the natural ebb and flow of the adventure, I can get in over my head and feel like I am drowning.

As I look out the window, watching and waiting for the first glimpse of land to be revealed by the receding ocean, I am reminded of what it feels like to be patient and wait until I know it is the right moment to make a move. I remember to trust this process of mindful waiting.

My prayer is that I could be in harmony with waiting in all areas of my life, knowing that the passage will appear when the time is right, just like this sandbar appears at low tide.

May you have the patience to wait for the
low tide moments in your life.
May you learn to slow down, to not push ahead,
to wait until the way is revealed.
May you trust that the way will present itself if
you stay mindful, patient and watchful.
May you find safe passage.

Sandbar

Splash

It is a beautiful November day and I am walking the beach. As I perch on a rock and watch the tide going out, my gaze wanders to the seals out in the cove. Like me, they are perched on rocks, enjoying the sun.

Suddenly, one seal slides off and splashes into the water. I can see his head bobbing around for a few moments. He climbs back up on the rock, sits for a moment and then slides back into the water with a splash.

I watch him as he plays. Over and over again, he climbs onto the rock and then slides off with a splash.

His antics make me laugh and remind me to be more playful in my own life. Just watching him delights me. I wonder, "How can I bring a splash of playfulness into my daily life?" The playfulness of this seal is refreshing. I realize, "This is what play does, it refreshes the spirit." As the seal settles back into stillness on his perch, I silently thank him for his teaching.

Go and play.

Persistence

Standing at the rim of the Grand Canyon, I am in awe. It is miles down to the Colorado River. From where I stand, I can just barely make out the ribbon of water flowing below. I have never seen anything like it and standing here makes my heart ache with something too deep for words.

Eventually, the word *persistence* rises to the surface of my awareness. I am gazing out at the evidence of what can happen when I have faith and hold my course in life. Persistence etches away the hard edges of stone. Persistence and holding my course can create beauty that astounds.

As I stand here, I recognize that I can give up too easily. When I don't immediately see results, I tend to allow doubt to lead me off course. This river is revealing the value of persistence. It seems to say, "Hold your course; keep all of your energy flowing in the direction you are called. Eventually, you will scratch the surface, you will break new ground and carve a path."

Be persistent.
Show up.
Have faith.
Keep flowing and make your beautiful creation.
Harness the power to flow like a river.
Trust the banks to hold you and help you maintain your course.
Persist.

Grand Canyon

Ripples

Standing at the river's edge, it is such a calm day, there is barely a hint of movement in the water. Then a breeze, like a soft exhale, whispers past me. I watch the water respond to the breeze with a gentle ripple that rolls away from me in a widening circle.

This gentle ripple reveals to me that change doesn't always have to come with turmoil and waves that stir life from its depths.

The smallest of actions that are as gentle as this breeze can have an impact that moves outward in ever-enlarging circles. Some days, smiling at a stranger can be an act of transformation. It is a mystery as to where these small acts can lead.

My soul yearns for this kind of gentle transformation. I've had enough of being tossed around in the tumultuous kind of change that turns life upside down. I welcome gentle changes and course adjustments. My soul responds to these gentle ripples with welcome.

Change me with gentleness, God.
I will respond to the softest whisper of your breath.

Watching the Fog Roll In

Sitting on the beach in Grand Manan, the sun is shining and makes the great Fundy waters sparkle. Yet, out on the horizon, I see a wall of grey moving across the water. The fog travels quickly, and I know it will not be long until it overtakes the landscape around me.

It is quite a sight to watch the fog roll in. It literally rolls across the ocean and up onto the land in great billows of fluffy, thick air. When the fog hits the land, it transforms everything. All the landmarks you know get swallowed up and become unrecognizable. The landscape is lost inside the grey and white mist.

For some reason, I find this comforting. Being swallowed up into the fog means it is a time to turn inward. This is not a day for sightseeing on the island. It is a day to stay close to our camp site and not wander off too far. The fog gives me a delicious excuse to curl up in a blanket with my journal and a mug of tea, perhaps even take a nap.

The appearance of the fog means it is once again a time of waiting and in that waiting, I have permission to nurture my inner life. I get to rest inside a cloud of stillness that invites me to pause, be slow, be gentle and trust small movements to get me where I need to go.

The Fog teaches patience.

Let Go and Flow

Out for a morning walk, I stop and pause as I cross a wooden bridge that spans a tidal river. As I watch the river flowing underneath me, I can tell the tide is going out and the river is returning water to the ocean.

The river flows with a fast current carrying logs, leaves and jelly fish as it passes under the bridge. As I watch, I hear the words, "Let the river carry you." This is an invitation to trust the current of life to carry me where I need to go. I stand there and watch two logs in the water. One is entrenched in the river bed, stuck and unable to move. The other log is floating freely, bobbing along the top of the water, effortlessly carried by the current.

The river is teaching me that as soon as I let go of needing to grasp and hold onto things, I am in flow. Flow is a state of acceptance and appreciation. When I simply stand back and appreciate where life is carrying me, there is no grasping, holding, strangling or struggling. I become the log being carried by the river, rather than the one mired down in the muddy water. Entering flow is the place of non-attachment and freedom: not attached to outcomes, not attached to anything – yet appreciating everything. This is the place of curiosity. Being able to observe life, be carried by it, and let it flow in, through and around me.

The river seems to say:

"Let go of your many worries, fears and fights.
Let the river of life carry you safely between its banks.
Let go and flow with the adventure that is your life.
Trust the current.
You are supported.
Let go."

Succulent Living

A number of years ago, I read a book called, *The School of Essential Ingredients*, by Erica Bauermeister. This book left me with a deep longing to learn how to live a succulent life; a life that is juicy, tasty, satisfying, and full of soul-nourishment.

Prior to reading this book, I had always associated the word *succulent* with the plants that are of a succulent variety, like a cactus. Succulent plants are able to retain their moisture in arid or dry conditions and I had not considered that my own life could be succulent.

Taking a vacation in Arizona brought me in contact with life in arid, desert-like conditions. The landscape was full of many varieties of succulent plants. These plants have thick skin that helps them retain their moisture and water to sustain life.

I was captivated by these plants. They are full of thorns, spikes and thistles, yet they are often the only beautiful spots of green in a vast landscape of brown and grey, stone and dust. These plants are resilient. They grow on the sides of rocky terrain as well as in arid, desert soil. I loved that they could retain their green aliveness in such dry conditions.

Standing in the desert, I was witnessing how life can remain moist, rich and nourishing on the inside, even when the landscape appears to be dry.

I have gone through dry periods in my life. At those times, my soul felt depleted and in need of nourishment and replenishment. I know what it feels like to be dry and barren inside - to feel like the desert landscape looks.

Over the past few years, I have been turning my attention and focus toward what makes my life feel succulent. What allows me to retain a sense of inner vitality and aliveness even when going through challenging times?

According to the dictionary[2], as an adjective, the word *succulent* means to be full of juice, to be rich in desirable qualities and to afford mental nourishment. For me, living a succulent life means ensuring that I have daily and weekly practices that give me nourishment. These practices include using my creativity, meditating daily, reading books that enrich my life and taking excursions that feed my soul. I have a morning practice of journaling and I have a daily practice of feeling and expressing gratitude for the big and small gifts that life has offered me throughout the day. Each of these practices helps me ensure that I am present to the life I am living. This act of being present to the moment is my key to living a succulent life. My daily practices help me notice that life is always trying to support me. My practices keep me connected to the awareness that no matter what is going on in the outer landscape of my life, I can choose to stay connected to that which nourishes me on the inside. On a daily basis, I must fill my inner well with soul-nourishing activities. I am learning not to make more withdrawals from this inner well than deposits. This is how I stay succulent.

Many years ago, Hildegard de Bingen, a twelfth-century Benedictine abbess, coined the phrase *veriditas* which means greening power. She knew that we must stay connected to the greening power of God to nourish the soul and keep our inner life moist and alive.

What makes your life succulent?

Cactus

Fire

A spark,
An ember,
A flame,
A blaze,
A light.

Let There be Light

When the conditions are right and sunlight passes through crystals in the air, a halo appears around the sun. The halo is caused by light refracting off the crystals and it creates this beautiful ring around the sun. When I see this, it brings to mind an image of the sun breathing, creating more space around itself in order to share its light.

I have seen a number of these sun halos this spring and it has made me think of how we can refract light into the world around us. Spring is a season when the heat of the sun is growing, warming the earth and calling forth new life and new beginnings in all of creation, including us.

There is a mantra that I enjoy using at this time of year, when I feel myself awakening from my winter hibernation. I simply recite the phrase, "Let there be light," during my morning meditation practice. I find this practice enlivening and it enhances my energy for the day. I feel more expansive after meditating with this mantra, as if my whole being is filled with light and radiating outward and refracting that light to the world around me.

> Let there be light in my mind and my consciousness.
> Let there be light in my heart and spirit.
> Let there be light in my solar plexus.
> Let there be light in my arms and hands.
> Let there be light in my legs and feet.

Let there be light in every cell of my being.
Let there be light in my thoughts.
Let there be light on my path as I move through the day.

Wherever you go this day, may you carry the light.
Wherever it is needed in the world this day, let there be light.

Fireflies

It is a beautiful summer evening and we are fortunate to be spending the weekend at my sister-in-law's cottage. It has been a warm day. The sun set a few hours ago and now the moon is shining a soft glow over the lake.

"Come over here," my brother-in-law calls in a loud whisper from the side veranda, "You've got to see this." We all come rushing over and then stop in our tracks. Hovering above the lawn are hundreds of tiny flickering lights flashing in the darkness. Fireflies dancing in the dark, making it feel like we have been transported to a fairy glen.

We stand in silent awe as we watch the show the fireflies are putting on for us. I marvel at the wonder of nature. The little sparks of light that are carried in the fireflies make me wonder if our soul light looks like that from the heavens. Do we look like sparks of light moving around on planet Earth?

So often, our gaze turns to the heavens to drink in the light of the stars, but do the stars look down on us and see us as flashes of illuminated light moving around on the earth?

I like to think so.

Touch of Light

The sun is filtering through my living room window and casts a warm glow on everything in the room. It is a gentle sun that enters softly, illuminating all that it touches. The orchid on the coffee table softly glows under the warmth of the light. The way the sun's rays settle across the room is romantic, as if I am watching a living love story, and I suppose I am. The whole room seems to be caressed by light and as I sit here, I suddenly feel so gently, yet greatly, loved. I am reminded of the words of a Kabbalistic saying that have been with me throughout this year: "Beside every blade of grass is an angel saying, 'Grow, grow, grow.' "[3]

As the sun touches my face, I suddenly feel the words of this saying take on life in my heart. The soft warmth of the light reminds me that tenderness and gentleness are qualities that call me to lean forward into life itself. They bring assurance and comfort, as well as strength and fortification.

As the sun shifts and the magic moment changes, I am left with the word *benevolence* in my heart. This is not a word I use every day, but I generally know the meaning of it as a desire to do good and to act with kindness.

This encounter with the sun has somehow softened my heart and branded it with the rich meaning of benevolence. I wonder where we ever got the idea that anything grows under the harsh glare of criticism

---

[3] Silver, Tosha. *Outrageous Openness: Letting the Divine Take the Lead.* New York, New York: Atria Paperback, 2015.

or judgement. I watch some of the reality shows on TV these days and my soul withers when I hear some of the remarks that "judges" offer contestants. What has made us think that speaking to one another and, perhaps more important, speaking to ourselves with harshness and criticism is the best way to help us grow into our potential? Judgement and criticism shrivel the soul, rather than call it to life.

May you feel the warmth of the light that calls you to grow.
May you be kind to yourself and speak to yourself
with gentleness, compassion and understanding.
May you shine the light of benevolence upon yourself and then
allow it to radiate outward to embrace the world around you.

Who knows? Through tenderness and loving kindness, we just might change the world.

Orchid

Solstice

A friend is having a gathering of women at her house for the winter solstice. We come together in her living room, gathered around the warm, crackling fire she has burning in the fireplace. The room is filled with the rich aroma of spicy, mulled wine and we munch on appetizers as we chat.

Eventually, the conversation quiets down, and the host turns to me, asking if I would lead the group in a meditation around the solstice. This is spur of the moment, but I feel inspired to agree.

I invite the women to stand and allow their gaze to settle upon the fire and then, when they are ready, to close their eyes and bring their awareness inside their bodies. I invite them to notice how it feels to be standing in this room, to notice the support of the floor beneath their feet, to notice the warmth of the fire and the companionship of this group.

Then I invite them to bring their awareness to their abdomen, to notice the warmth of their inner fire and inner light. I ask them to sense their inner fire and to notice how it is burning. Is it a roaring fire, filled with energy and vitality? Is it a small flicker of a flame that softly glows? Or is it warm embers, glowing red and hot?

As we stand together on this darkest night, preparing to invite the light back into our days, I invite us all to simply notice our inner light, to try not to change it in any way, but instead to ask it what it needs from us right now. What does this inner light, inner fire need to sustain it? How does it want to be nurtured?

After a moment of silence, I encourage them to thank whatever their inner light has shared with them. I invite them to thank the energy of their inner fire, to let it know they are there to tend this fire and to nurture it in the days ahead.

May we be attentive keepers of our inner fire, our inner light that glows and contributes to the light of the world.

Cabin Fever

There is something about the month of February that elicits a sense of boredom and restlessness within me. I have a need to get outdoors more, yet the snowbanks are so high that it is a challenge to do much outside. This restlessness brings with it a sense of irritation. Wanting to get moving - and not being able to - creates a sense of restriction. The feeling of boredom comes from being limited in the activities I can do and being unable to get outside and go for long walks as much as I would like.

All of this combines to create not only irritation, but impatience. These two feelings make me decidedly unsettled because I want things to be different than they are. I am ready to sit outside and feel the breeze on my face and hear the sound of birds singing instead of sitting by my fire, reading, while it snows.

This long winter is helping me learn to embrace a state of patience and enter, willingly, into a place of waiting. Patience leads me to drop into the present moment and connect to the beauty of winter that surrounds me. When I stop wanting things to be different than they are and I simply accept what is, then the restless feeling begins to dissipate and a state of calm enters.

I am reminded of something I heard Mary Morrissey share in her Quantum Leap program that helps me move into a place of acceptance. She said that when we can create a sense of enthusiasm for the conditions we are currently in, we become engaged with life. I take this to mean that enthusiasm feeds the inner fire of the soul and generates energy, just like adding coal to a fire provides fuel for the flame. Interestingly, the root word of enthusiasm is *entheos*, meaning God within; or to put it another way, it means to look for the Good within the situation.[4] When I apply this simple lesson to my feelings about this wintery month, I reconnect to the beauty that surrounds me.

When the snow stops falling, I go out to shovel. As I scoop up piles of snow in the curve of the shovel, the snow looks so white that it is almost blue. It is a stunning and captivating colour. The wind blows on my face and, because the snowbanks rise above my head, I am trying to heave the shovel as high as I can to get the snow over the top of the banks. As I move piles of snow, I connect to the fact that my shovel is filled to brimming with individual and unique snowflakes. No two snowflakes are exactly the same, and to imagine the number of unique snowflakes filling my yard is truly astounding. Before long, as I shovel, I am awestruck by the wonder of it all. The snow suddenly represents piles and piles of unique creations and it makes me wish I had the kind of creativity that puts out this much abundance. I fall back in love with the snow and its beauty. My irritation, restlessness and boredom dissolve completely.

When we find something that we can become enthused about in our current situation, when we can begin to see the good in it, we raise our happiness factor and move into a state of harmony and well-being. Connecting with enthusiasm gives us more energy, rather than lulling us into complacency or irritation. By the time I finished with my shoveling, I felt enlivened and brimming with creative energy. I was once again inspired and ready to go back inside the house and do some writing.

May you fan the flame of enthusiasm within you this day.

---

[4] Although not an exact quote, Mary Morrissey inspired this reflection on enthusiasm. Inspired from Quantum Leap of LifeSOULutions That Work, LLC. More info here: www.marymorrissey.com

Insight

It has been a long day of working at my computer and I need to get up and go for a walk because I am stuck and in need of inspiration. As I wander through my neighborhood, I consider the idea that there is great value in analytical thinking, but innovative solutions come from beyond the analytical mind.

Einstein knew we needed more than just the analytical mind; he knew we needed to learn how to let go and *allow* something new to *find us*. He would go for walks and spend time in nature to make space for sparks of creativity to find him.

This is dancing with creativity.

We open to allow the flame of inspiration to find us and give us new awareness – flashes of insight we have never considered before.

Yielding

It has been a long winter, and spring is trying hard to break winter's hold on the land. The sun is getting warmer every day and the snow is gently yielding to the heat of the sun.

As I go out for walks and even as I sit in my office to write, I can hear the sounds of the snow yielding to the penetrating warmth of the sun. I hear little rivulets of water trickling down from my roof and flowing along the streets. These trickling sounds are evidence that the snow is surrendering to the changing of the seasons. It is time to transition from winter to spring and the snow must surrender its frozen state so that it is once again flowing water.

There is a divine dance between the sun and water that the cycles of the seasons reveal. The heat of the sun helps form and shape the water. In the summer months, the sun keeps the water fluid and moving in the rivers and lakes. On a hot day, the sun evaporates water, lifting it up until it accumulates as clouds in the sky that eventually release and disperse rain across the face of the earth. In the cold of winter, when the sun does not rise as high, the clouds release multitudes of snowflakes, each one an individual design, custom made and unique.

This year, we have had an abundance of snow. I imagine the individual crystals changing from their solid state back into water as they melt. I envision them letting go and returning back to the rivers and the oceans from all over the land and becoming part of the larger whole again.

This is what yielding does - it allows us to surrender, to merge, to let go and become one with life. Listening to the snow yielding its frozen state under the increasing heat of the sun reminds me that nothing stays the same forever: we are always in flux and flow with the cycles of life.

I listen to the sound of the snow melting and recognize that something is happening in the outer world that echoes within my soul and makes me think of letting go of the resistance that lives inside of me. Resistance to change or resistance to growth creates a frozen state, a holding pattern, within the body. Resistance creates a state of tension that stops the natural flow of life and makes my body stiff and inflexible.

Yet, I know that if I trust that resistance exists for a reason, and it is simply showing up because some part of me is afraid of the unknown and needs some reassurance, then I begin to relax. When I turn the gentle gaze of compassion upon resistance, it yields and melts away. There are many things that melt resistance: compassion, love, understanding, and reassurance act just like the warmth of the sun on snow. These qualities melt and transform inner resistance into life energy that helps us return to a state of flow and freedom.

When dealing with resistance, compassion brings reassurance that feels as comforting as the warmth of the sun. Tension yields and melts away under the kind gaze of compassion, returning the life within to a natural state of fluid movement.

Listening to the trickling water, I hear the music of the divine dance of life beckoning: "Come and join in. It's time to melt."

Good Company

It is a chilly, spring evening and I have just laid the fire in the front room of the house in Castlemartyr. One thing I have come to appreciate during my time in Ireland is the laying of the fire in the evening and the slow, penetrating warmth that chases the damp away.

The light of this fire has begun to dance in the room and brings with it a cheerful animation that makes me want to curl up beside it. This is the first fire I have tended since I arrived to visit my friend. Most nights, I have watched her prepare the fire for the evening. Tonight, she asked if I would do it and I must say, there is something satisfying about being the keeper of the fire this evening. It feels like a responsibility to be the one to strike the match that ignites the flame that warms the room and sends images of flames dancing across the floor and the walls.

When my friend walks into the room and sees me gazing at the fire, she says, "The fire is good company isn't it?"

I hadn't thought of it that way before, but it is true. The fire has its own sounds and movements that make the room feel brighter, fuller and warmer. Its presence captures my attention and keeps me engaged with it for hours. The evening fire is why I love camping so much. There is nothing like sitting around a campfire late into the night and watching the logs slowly burn, sending off sparks and light in a glowing circle. The flames are captivating and mesmerizing.

Indeed, a fire is good company that chases the dark away and it makes me think of the generations of people it has kept warm and fed across the ages. Fire is more than good company; it is a gift of life.

Perhaps the next time you light a candle, or strike a match, you might give thanks for the gift of the flame.

For this flame of life, I offer my thanks.
For this circle of warmth, I offer my thanks.
For the light that illuminates the darkness, I offer my thanks.

Revelation

It's a foggy morning and my husband and I are walking on the beach. The penetrating heat of the sun is slowly burning off the fog as we walk. I like the feeling of being held inside the fog and not being able to see very far in front of me or across the water. I decide to let my husband walk on without me as I sit on a rock to watch what happens as the fog begins to lift and dissipate.

As the sun rises higher in the sky, the fog thins and the view begins to shift and change so suddenly that I am awestruck. The water shimmers and sparkles with sunlight as the landscape begins to brighten. Where there was nothing but mist, suddenly the tip of a sail comes into view. In my peripheral vision, a majestic cliff emerges as if by magic and I turn to my left to look at it. The stunning beauty of these surprises takes my breath away. In moments, all that was once unseen makes itself visible and I am delighted. I am sitting inside a process of revelation.

As I observe the sun dispersing the fog, it feels like Spirit is showing me that this is how fast life changes. What was invisible can become visible right before your eyes and what was visible can also disappear right before your eyes. The world is constantly shifting, changing, coming into and moving out of form.

In that moment, I felt the invitation from Spirit to move in this fluid manner in my life; to allow things in and out of my awareness and in and out of my physical surroundings as well.

There's a lesson here for me about letting go. As I release what is familiar to me, something new will be made known.

As I watch the sun and fog interact, I get a visual sense of what happens in the process of change. Nothing stays the same forever; life is constantly shifting into and out of form. At times, my invitation is to just sit, watch and do nothing as the fog gives itself over to the heat of the sun and the way forward is revealed. Things will become clear, just like the cliff suddenly came into my field of vision where moments before nothing but a hazy mist seemed to exist.

Often, I have found myself saying the words, "I just don't know what to do." These words are my indicator to come fully into the present moment and look around me to see if a path is becoming visible. I must look for just one step I can take. If that step is not visible to me, then my job is to wait and allow clarity to find me. My job is to sit in the mist, to be still in the very midst of the mystery of God and allow the sun to rise. All will be made known in its own time and in its own way.

You cannot push the fog away; it does not work that way. In moments of uncertainty, all I can do is find my inner point of stillness, open myself to the present moment, and *allow* the way to be revealed.

Allowing the answers to find me, allowing the clarity to find me is the key. It only happens when I find my resting place within. When I, metaphorically, sit on a rock on the beach, fully awake and alert to my surroundings, waiting, and watching, the way will be revealed.

On Beauty

It is a glorious day to be at the beach. The sun is shining, children are playing in the water while parents watch from the beach, shorebirds are wandering across the sand, and the blue Fundy waters stretch before us. My heart expands and I am struck by the beauty of it all. At the same time, I wonder how many of the people on this beach truly recognize their own beauty. One of the biggest challenges many of us face is to accept and appreciate our own beauty.

Too often, we are consumed with feelings of not being good enough. For beauty to be revealed, we must commit to doing the inner work of excavating false beliefs that stop us from embracing the depths of our capacity to love, so that we might shine the light of love on ourselves and others.

This excavation work is a journey from fear to love.
A journey of letting go of what others think of us.
A journey of allowing ourselves to be seen.
A journey of accepting ourselves from the inside out.

Life is precious. From the moment of birth, we illuminate beauty, but too often the outside voices intrude and make us believe we are anything other than perfect exactly as we are. The innermost part of ourselves that carries our soul light is pure love. We cause ourselves pain and suffering when we cannot see this.

Learning to see and accept our beauty, rather than be caught in habitual cycles of counting our faults, is not an easy task. It takes a willingness to see and accept our talents, our gifts, and our capacity to love in order to embrace the unique expression of life that we are. It takes tenacity and willingness to move from self-rejection to self-acceptance and to allow our inner light to become even more radiant so that it can shine out into the world as a love that embraces, accepts and honours the beauty inherent in all living things.

A number of years ago, I created this mandala. When I was done creating it, the name "Beauty Unveiled" came to me along with the words:

Gaze out into the world with eyes of love and beauty is revealed.
Gaze inward upon yourself with eyes of love and beauty is unveiled.

Mandala

    May these words touch your heart and help you to see your own light and beauty. May you no longer hide your light under a bushel, but allow it to shine so the whole world can benefit from the beauty that is YOU.

"You are the light of the world."
Matthew 5:14

Air

A breeze,
A wind,
A gust,
A gale,
A force.

An inhale.
An exhale.

Breath of Life.

Witnessing the Sunset

Going for drives during the summer months is quite a beautiful experience in the Maritimes. You will notice people communing with nature in very simple ways. Today, I saw a man sitting on a lawn chair in front of his open garage door. His car was parked in the garage behind him and he had a lovely view of the ocean from his chair. He was simply staring out at the setting sun, taking in the colour and the beauty of it.

Driving past him and witnessing his serene pose and contemplative stature made my heart widen with a sense of peace, like I had just seen an everyday mystic sitting in that chair. This was someone who was called outdoors by beauty and who pulled up a chair to view the sunset as his evening entertainment rather than watch TV. The memory of him sitting there, with quiet reverence before the setting sun, is etched into my mind.

This man didn't know he was inspiring me as he watched the sun set. Yet seeing that he had taken a moment to pause, pull up a chair and drink in the beauty of the setting sun spoke volumes to me about how to live a meaningful and connected life. He reminded me to slow down and appreciate the beauty around me. He inspired me to remain committed to knowing there is no greater show I could be viewing than the one that nature puts on for me every day.

Witnessing the actions of this everyday mystic said to me, "Don't miss the depth hidden in simplicity, for it is the simple things that can call us into the very heartbeat of Life."

In what ways are you inspired by the simple things in life? What brings a smile to your face, warmth to your heart, and enlivens your senses?

Sunset

Winds of Change

It is while visiting my brother and sister-in-law in Dubai and experiencing the desert for the first time that I truly understand the expression "the winds of change."

I stare out at the desert dunes and see them shifting before my eyes. The breath of the wind is transforming the dunes, continuously reforming them throughout the day. It is a gentle reshaping and reformation, yet I can also sense that a true windstorm would have you lost in no time. The landscape would change that quickly.

Yet this gentle shifting I am witnessing feels almost magical and comforting. It makes me realize that change really is happening all of the time.

Often, we fear change, yet the desert teaches me that we can actually rely on it, in a good way. The winds of change are continually active in our lives. No matter what is happening in our life right now, it can and will shift into something new.

We are never truly stuck. The winds of change will always reform, reshape and transform the world within and around us.

The Wind Dance

The sound of a river rushing by caught me by surprise and I turned to see that it was actually the voice of the wind playing with the leaves of a tree. This realization made me smile and I acknowledged the wind and the way it can mimic other sounds in nature. The wind has a voice of its own and it uses this voice in many different expressions. What I have noticed though, is that the wind makes the most unique sounds when it is rubbing up against something else. All on its own, the wind can be almost silent. When it dances across the path of a tree, however, it creates music and harmony with the leaves. When the wind blows across the windows of my home, it whistles; when it bounces off the walls of a cave, its echoes call to me.

I love the voice of the wind. It is dynamic and changes with everything that it touches. I love that the wind not only has a sound; it also has a feel. On a warm summer day, it can come as a light and refreshing breeze that caresses my skin. On a winter day, it comes with a force that stings my cheeks and makes my forehead ache. At any moment, the touch of the wind may shift and feel different to me.

Each of us can also play with the music of the wind with our own voice. It is only the force of air moving across our vocal cords that allows us to make sounds. We can control how loud or soft the sound is by how we use the air that is breathing us.

Wind, air, breath, they are all the same thing. They all have a voice. They all have a touch. The impact of their voice depends on the force with which they blow. As I make myself an instrument for the wind to play through and allow the air to breathe through me, I am partaking in a dance with the universe. I am co-creating and making music with my voice, my breath, my being. I choose to make the dance a peaceful one today. I choose to allow my breath to be soft. I choose to allow the wind of my voice to create currents of love that ripple into the universe.

Each day, I can choose how I want to interact and play with the wind. What impact do I want to have on the world around me? The wind and I are partners in this dance of life. I am an instrument for the wind. Just like the leaves of the tree I walked past, the wind plays a song with my voice and with my life. This day, I pray I make the song a beautiful one.

"I am but a feather on the breath of God."
~Hildegard de Bingen~

Feather

Rhythms

The wind teaches us a rhythm in life and so does the heat. When it is really hot, humid and muggy outside, we slow down. When the air is still, we slow down. We cannot move as fast when there is not a breeze to support us. Perhaps the wind keeps the energy within and around us moving so that we can undertake the daily tasks that make up our lives.

These past few days when the air has been still, hot and humid, it has been hard to breathe. It has been a challenge to undertake the daily chores that need to be done. The air lulls me into stillness. It calls me to go deeper, to conserve my energy and to move wisely.

This is my lesson today: to move wisely rather than frantically. Moving wisely means that I listen and am in tune with my body and move at the pace that it can handle. Moving wisely means that my actions match my highest priorities for my life.

"Nature does not hurry, yet everything is accomplished."
~Lao Tzu~

Quietness of Being

A deep longing for quiet has lured me out into nature this morning. It is not so much the sound of quiet I am yearning for, but a longing for an internal quietness of being that has brought me out here to sit by the ocean. My spirit longs for an inner quiet that allows me to catch my breath.

Here, by the water's edge, with the trees at my back and the sun on my face, my breath deepens. My chest relaxes and opens. As I watch the birds soaring in the sky, the noise of the world drops away and I begin to feel a quietness of heart and mind come over me. It is a relief to enter into the silence of pure presence and experience the blessing of non-doing.

Later in the day, I talk with a friend about this yearning for quiet and these words come to me:

A Quietness of Being

Set down the tasks.
Set down the doing.
Rest awhile in the silence of the heart.
The silence where all things dwell.
The quiet place that is not empty, but is full of emptiness.

The place of quiet depth of being.
Deep quiet.
Deep spaciousness.

The quiet that lies at the center of all things.
Listen and be with that sense of quiet.
Appreciate the quiet of your being.

Once again, I am reminded that St. Augustine once said that God's first language is silence. On a day like today, I know this to be true. It is in this deep quiet that I commune with the Sacred. It is a place too deep for words.

Lake

Tenacity of the Soul

It is a windy day, the kind where the wind whistles and howls through the windows. I am sitting at my kitchen table, eating my lunch and watching the wind toss the branches of the maple tree in my backyard. It is springtime; the leaves are tender and new, and this wind seems determined to tear them from the branches.

In the midst of the wind, a monarch butterfly lands on a leaf. It is hanging upside down and I find myself transfixed as I watch it. Gusts of wind whip the branches around, but this delicate butterfly holds fast to its leaf.

Butterflies have always had a special meaning for me. I appreciate their capacity to undergo such a complete transformation in order to become a creature of lightness and beauty. As I watch this particular creature from my window, I notice something about the butterfly that I had not seen before; there is an amazing strength within these delicate beings.

As I watch the butterfly defy the force of the wind, I remember something I had come across in my research about labyrinths; *butterfly* and *soul* were the same word in the ancient Greek language: *psyche*. Something about this realization, married to the image of this butterfly hanging onto a leaf in the blowing wind, makes me aware of the strength that abides within the human soul. I have, at times, thought of my soul as being tender and delicate and in need of protection, yet I know that there are times in my life when it is the tenacity and strength of my soul that has pulled me through.

The soul is not as delicate as I sometimes think it is. Just like this butterfly, the soul knows how to hang on in the tough times of depression, anxiety, chaos and confusion that often lead to our own surrender and transformation. When life seems to be falling apart all around and gales of wind are blowing, the soul knows its purpose and is able to hold on through the storm.

It intrigues me that there is a connection between the words *soul*, *butterfly* and *psyche* in ancient Greek. In our modern day, we have come to think of psyche as the mind, but the inclusion of the soul in the word's meaning reminds me of our capacity to transform ourselves and our lives to live in accordance with our very essence - the truth that lies buried at the core of who we are.

I think of the transformative process which the caterpillar must undergo to gain its wings to become a butterfly like the one I am watching. The caterpillar must surrender itself completely to the process of transformation. Written right into the DNA of the caterpillar is the grand design for the butterfly and the transformative process it undergoes. This process knows exactly when the caterpillar must begin wrapping itself in a cocoon to prepare for its metamorphosis. The caterpillar knows how to surrender itself completely to the transformative process.

This potential for *becoming* is hidden in the DNA of everything on the planet and it is encoded in each of us. The mystic Teilhard de Chardin called the seed of our potential *entelechy*, the force within us that is waiting to be unlocked and realized.

These reflections give me solace and let me know that, just like the butterfly hanging onto the leaf, there is a strength far greater than me that animates my life and informs me of the steps to take in my transformative journey. It is my job to create the spaces and places that are safe enough for me to hear the voice of my soul, the voice that is connected to the Divine, and to respect the needs, desires and impulses that arise from this place that is bigger, vaster and stronger than I will ever fully know.

Like the butterfly instinctively maintaining its hold on a leaf in the midst of a windstorm, the soul knows what to do to sustain life; its grip is tenacious, even in the midst of adversity. For me, this is what it means to surrender my will to God's will. It is to surrender the need for struggle and strife that arises during periods of transformation and to sink inward, to listen to the spark of the Divine within me in order to know what to do. These periods of change can feel like a time of tremendous loss, when what I once knew is shaken up or stripped away and what is left feels unfamiliar, new and vulnerable.

It is through the spiritual practices of prayer, meditation, and spiritual direction that I create the cocoon that helps me discover what steps to take in my transformative journey. Sometimes, that step is to simply hang on until the wind settles.

What helps you weather the winds of change and transformation?

Blown Open

It was a blustery night. The wind was battering against the house and I could hear the branches of the cedar trees scraping the roof. So many noises accompany a wind that gusts this strong. It makes the house groan as if it is using all of its stamina to stand intact against the force of the wind.

I lay in bed and listen to the wind wrestling with the house and the trees outside. It is as if the wind has a desire to make a lasting impression by changing the landscape throughout the night.

When I wake in the morning and look out my kitchen window, I see that the wind has had its way. Two portions of my fence have been blown apart, leaving a gaping hole into the neighbour's yard. As I take in this new image of my fence, the words, "the gate has opened," come to me.

My pulse quickens with that thought.

For months, I have felt like I am sitting in front of a closed gate, patiently waiting. I know that the gate represents a new portion of my life that is about to open. I can feel it in my bones. I am ready to cross over a threshold into something new.

Somehow, in the middle of the night, the wind has come to my aid. It has blown the gate wide open.

I am thankful that it is winter and we will not be able to fix our fence until the spring. I enjoy standing in my kitchen window and looking out at this gate the wind has created for me. This image reinforces the feeling deep inside that the way forward has been cleared, the waiting is over.

The gate has opened. It took a force larger than myself to open the gate. It took the breath of the wind.

All of this reminds me that there is a time for everything. It reminds me that there are forces in life that will come to my aid and help me. I don't have to do everything by myself. Sometimes, patience is the way forward. I can wait and trust the natural force of life will blow in such a way that the path forward opens itself.

An unexpected gate has opened in my fence, but it has also opened in my heart. Once again, the outer world reflects an inner movement happening in my soul. It brings me peace.

Through what seems like destruction, new life is beckoning.
The fence has broken open.
The boundaries have expanded.
You can step beyond where you have been.

Wind at My Back

I am out for my morning walk and the wind is blowing fierce and hard. It feels nice as I walk downhill and the wind is at my back. I feel assisted by the wind as it naturally accelerates my pace and practically carries me down the hill with its momentum.

That changes when I turn and begin my walk back home. Now I am walking uphill, heading directly into the power of the wind. It suddenly feels like I am trying to walk through molasses as the force of the wind slows each step. The wind has become a force pushing against me, and I have to fight for each forward moving step.

As I walk into the wind, I realize that this is exactly what it feels like when I encounter my own resistance. When I am working on a project and resistance rises up within me, it almost stops me in my tracks, and I have to fight for every inch of progress that I make. Resistance slows me down and makes the work a struggle. Resistance is like walking into a strong wind. It is like wrestling with an unseen force with the power to knock me over at any moment.

I have noticed that there are times when the closer I get to a goal, the stronger the wind of my internal resistance seems to blow. I know that this resistance is my ego working to protect me and keep me safe from the change it feels is imminent if I achieve my goal. Resistance does not like change and fights to maintain the status quo. Grappling with resistance can be exhausting, and my walk with the wind this morning makes me think that there must be an easier way.

When I walk with the wind at my back, the wind assists me in making progress. When I walk into the wind, I am battling to hold my ground.

Resistance can be a tricky thing. I have learned that the stronger the internal resistance is, the more it is a sign that I am moving in the right direction. It wouldn't try so hard to stop me if I wasn't getting close. When resistance rises up like the force of this wind, I must hunker down and be dogged in my progress. I must face the intense wind of resistance by pulling my hat down more securely on my head, keeping my eyes on my path and taking one slow step at a time.

It is ironic that, walking into the headwind, I know I am on the right path. As much as resistance pushes against me, I know that it is the guiding force that is leading me home.

When facing the gales of a headwind,
may courage rise to your aid,
and turn resistance into an ally,
helping you overcome adversity,
procrastination,
and doubt.
May resistance turn into persistence,
and guide you to your goal.
For resistance is merely a training ground,
for the tenacity of the soul.

The Quiet of the Forest

Some colleagues have invited me to a silent winter retreat. I arrive in the late afternoon, eager to enter these few days of quiet. I have forgotten what a relief it can be to spend time in community in silence – no need to speak, no expectation to make conversation, just an invitation to enter into quiet presence.

Once I have settled my things in my room, I go for a walk around the grounds. It is a beautiful winter day, the kind where the snow glistens, but the air is still. I find the trail that I know will take me into the woods and begin to follow it. I have taken a walking stick with me as I expect it to be icy in spots. What I haven't expected is for the snow to be packed so hard that it feels like walking onto a skating rink. I am grateful to have the walking stick as my companion.

My first few minutes on the trail take me up a hill and into the woods. When I reach the top, I stop. I breathe. I listen.

There is nothing like the quiet of the forest on a calm winter day. There is no sound, no wind, just the feel of refreshing cold air on my face. The quiet touches my heart. I have been waiting for this - the deep quiet of nature.

I turn my face up to take in the sight of the trees. Wonderful friends. They know what quiet is. They spend much of their lives quietly standing tall, witnessing the world around them. I smile and say hello.

One tree in particular is shedding its bark in large, loose curls that haven't quite fallen off, but are hanging raggedly from its trunk. Layers falling away. Releasing what is not needed. Freeing the tender bark that lies underneath the rough surface.

This tree provides a living image of what silent retreat feels like to me. It is a time of releasing, of letting the outer layers peel back to reveal a softer, subtler part of me. I thank the tree for the visual it offers to represent an inner process that I find hard to articulate. It seems to welcome me and prepare the way into my retreat time.

I stand under its branches for a moment and simply listen to the quiet. I have been aching for this, the deep quiet of the forest in winter, snow insulating and muffling all sounds.

A forest at rest.
A deep quiet.
Turning inward.
Stillness of being.
No words to describe it.
Just impressions on the heart.
Smiling.
Joy bubbling to the surface.
A feeling of home.
Being welcomed by towering friends,
welcomed into their silence.
Returning to a way of being,
that is more natural than breathing.
Sighing.
Content.
There is nothing like the deep quiet of the forest in winter.

Strengthened by Stillness

This morning, nature is reflecting back to me something for which I have been longing. I yearn for stillness.

Everything is still as I sit on my front deck. Even when I went for my morning walk, there was a hush about the world around me that was so welcome. It helped me to drop down inside myself so that I could connect to my own inner stillness.

The air was so calm that there was barely a suggestion of a breeze. Nothing moved. The trees had stopped swaying and their leaves were hanging still. The flowers stood tall and motionless, with nothing to disturb them, not even cars passing by. Even the spider hanging upside down in its web in the tree in front of me is perfectly still and at rest.

Normally, on a hot summer morning, I would find this kind of stillness oppressive. On this morning, however, I find that the serenity offers a welcome invitation. The stillness of the flowers, the grasses, and the trees shows me what it is to be in a peaceful resting place.

There is deep quiet in the neighborhood, as though the mugginess and stillness of the world around us has lulled all humans into the presence of silence.

This stillness is not stagnant. It is a pregnant pause in which I can relax long enough for all the scattered energy and pieces of myself to find their way home. Stillness feels good. It invites me to find my center point and to move slowly, deliberately.

As I allow the humid, still heat of the day to permeate my being, I feel a sense of being recharged. I want to smile for no reason. My ears are awakening to the hum of bees in the flowers and the song of cardinals in the trees. In this stillness, I am becoming more aware of the subtle movements of life within and around me. This is the place of calm and peace.

The weather predictions call for thunderstorms later in the day. There is a reason that there is a calm before a storm. It is in the stillness that we gather our strength.

In the stillness I am reminded of the Psalm 46:10 and the prayer that goes with it.

"Be still and know that I am God!"
Psalm 46:10

Be still and know that I am God.
Be still and know that I Am.
Be still and know.
Be still.
Be.

Acknowledgements

There have been many helping hands involved in nurturing and creating this book, and I send out my gratitude to all who have taken part in this project.

To my husband, who has been so patient and encouraging throughout the unfolding process of compiling these reflections: you have encouraged me for years to share my writing. Thank you for your willingness to read everything I write, for telling me it's beautiful and to keep on going. You have believed in my ability to write messages that inspire and touch the heart long before I was willing to believe in myself. I am ever grateful to be your wife and to share my life with you.

To my mom, Myrna, who has always believed in me and continues to be my biggest fan: thank you for your hours of proofreading, editing and offering suggestions to make the reflections in this book the best they can be. You have been a steady source of encouragement throughout my life and I thank you for your patient and steadfast belief in my abilities.

To my step-mom, Candy: how do I thank you for the support and encouragement to create this book? You kept telling me that you would love to have a book of short reflections that you might read as you start or end your day. You have honestly and thoughtfully given me your feedback on everything I have written and you help make it better. So here is the book that you have been asking for all these years. Thank you for helping me through the creation process.

To my aunt, Tammy: thank you for the gift of your artwork that graces the cover of this book. Your creativity, patience and curiosity toward life have always inspired me. Whether growing flowers in your backyard, painting, or making pottery, you exude a sense of wonder, surprise and delight over the outcome. You nurture life in so many ways and have nurtured mine in more ways than you know.

There are many friends who have supported me through the process of writing this book. Beth and Mary, my heart is full of gratitude for each of you. You have been there to read much of my writing and your encouragement has helped me gain the confidence to compile and share these reflections with others. Karen, thank you for your enthusiasm for this project and for helping me write copy for the cover of the book. Laura L., thank you for being my Focusing and writing partner and for being there when there are writing emergencies! Laura K., thank you for so graciously providing your editing skills to support this venture.

I send out a prayer of gratitude to my dear friend, Charlotte: you are no longer here to hold this book in your hands, yet I have felt your presence near me every step of the way. I am grateful for the book you wrote before you left us. It is a gift that I turn to often for inspiration. We used to talk about the books we wanted to write. I received yours five years ago; well, here is mine, my friend. Wherever you are, I know you are smiling on me and celebrating with me.

Finally, this book would never have been born if it weren't for the generous gifts of nature. It is to you that I turn every day to restore my heart, strengthen my spirit and inspire my creativity. It is through the beauty of nature that I sense the radiance of the Sacred embracing, guiding and comforting me through the ordinary and extraordinary moments of living. As an expression of my gratitude, a portion of the proceeds of this book will be donated to organizations dedicated to preserving and honoring nature's gifts.

Printed in the United States
By Bookmasters